746.44

D0581166

TEXTURES IN EMBROIDERY

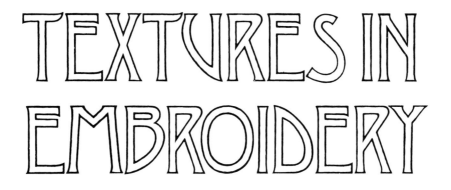

TEXTURES IN EMBROIDERY

VALERIE CAMPBELL-HARDING

B T Batsford Ltd London

ISBN 0 7134 4625 0

Filmset in 10/12pt. 'Monophoto' Century
Schoolbook
by Servis Filmsetting Limited, Manchester

Printed & bound in Great Britain by
Anchor Brendon Ltd, Tiptree, Essex
for the publishers B T Batsford Limited
4 Fitzhardinge Street, London W1H 0AH

CONTENTS

ACKNOWLEDGMENTS

I should like to thank Margaret Barr, Jan Beany, Jane Clarke, Jane Lemon, Jan Messent, Nancy Robertson, Audrey Walker, and Sarah, Jonathan and Paul Harding for allowing me to photograph their work. Also my thanks to Peter Francis for taking the colour photographs.

My gratitude goes to E.K. Norris without whom I would never have become an embroiderer.

INTRODUCTION

Texture in embroidery means the almost limitless arrangement of threads, fabrics and other materials to create a finished piece of work that has tactile as well as visual appeal. Texture adds tonal qualities to colour. Roughness gives a greater variety of tone than smoothness because of the shadows and highlights on the uneven surface.

To carry out a design, purely orthodox or traditional methods are not sufficient, and imagination is valued more than technical skill alone. Good technique is necessary, and no pains should be spared to achieve this, but ingenuity in the use of materials as well as in the design intrigues and stimulates the observer and captures his interest, which technique by itself cannot do.

Embroidery is constantly changing, and outside influences from many sources blend with accepted ideas to compel techniques to expand. Discovery of something new through investigation into stitches and methods is not only interesting but avoids a watering down of fashionable ideas and ensures that the personality of the embroiderer projects through the final result. Much thought should go into what can be done with the many materials available and the various effects that can be achieved with them in order to convey the subject matter in the best way. A collection of trials and samplers should be built up to use as reference, to familiarize the fingers in the handling of different materials and to sort out one's ideas when planning a large piece of work (figures 1, 2 and 3). Continual experimenting is necessary to avoid repetition; some failures are inevitable, but one can learn as much from failure as from success. These samplers are not an end in themselves but are investigatory studies only, and they should have a specific purpose in view.

One way of experimenting to find new textures is to look at other surfaces, patterns and textures (figure 4) not normally associated with embroidery, and to try and achieve a similar effect with threads, fabrics or any other material that will produce the desired result. This may turn out not to be

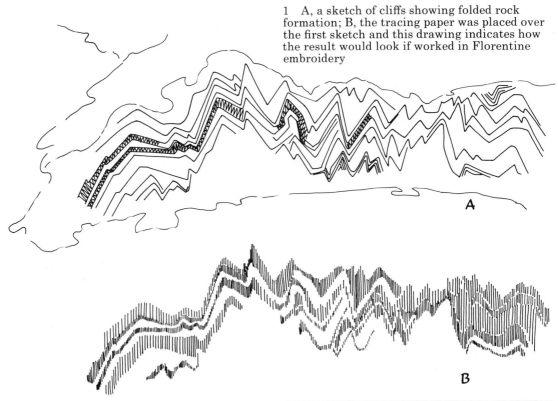

1 A, a sketch of cliffs showing folded rock formation; B, the tracing paper was placed over the first sketch and this drawing indicates how the result would look if worked in Florentine embroidery

relevant at the time, but it could well be just what is wanted for some future work. The more experience one has of how to obtain many different textures, the easier it is to find the right one for a particular place.

Samplers can be worked that explore the possibilities of one stitch and its variations, the best use of a new material or the different ways of attaching a found object. Other samplers could use materials, stitches or methods that are normally associated with a particular type of thread or embroidery in another context, such as canvas work in ribbon or cut purls. Two different types of embroidery can be combined, such as cut work and quilting (figures 5 and 6). Embroidery can be combined with other crafts, and provided that the inherent qualities of threads and fabrics are retained this can work very well. Some methods are more flexible than others for building up rich textures, and some are more suitable for interpreting specific ideas – these will be discovered by experience.

2 A trial was worked based on a small part of the drawing of cliffs shown in figure 1. Drawn threadwork, pulled work, knotted stitch, whipped threads and looped back stitch, using chenille, leather strips, perle and wools

8

3 Another trial was worked using fabrics laced
over thickly padded card. Small tassels were
made separately and added. The finished panel
will use elements from both these trials

4 Sketches of objects which could be interpreted in stitchery: A, a microscope slide of a mineral; B, fungus growing on a tree; C, a pattern on a moulded glass tumbler; D, human muscles; E, stalactites; F, pulled toffee; G, a tracing of a rubbing of a shell (the paper was moved at intervals during the rubbing); H, a part of the cross-section of a lime tree; I, growth patterns on a diamond crystal; J, the underside of a mushroom

5 *opposite* 'African Village' by Nancy Robertson. The top part of the canvas was lightly sprayed with silver, and the canvas stitches worked in grey–blue, gold and old rose wools allowing some of the canvas to show through. Surface stitches were worked on top in fine black thread

6 A detail of 'African Village'

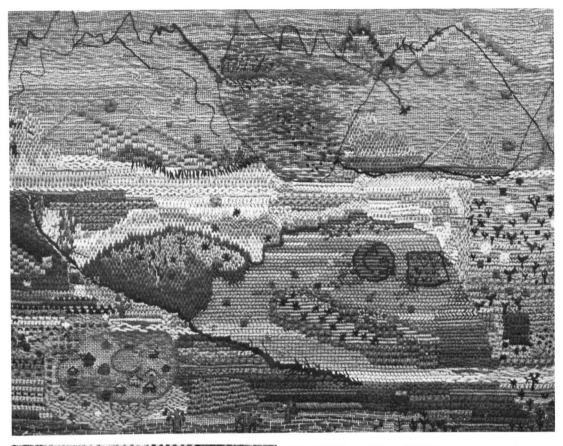

SPACES AND LINES

Broadly speaking there are two main problems when deciding how to carry out a design. One is how to fill a space, and the other is how to get from one place to another. When planning the treatment, whichever method is used, it is helpful to indicate the direction of the threads; it is also useful to show whether the lines are straight, curved or wavy and whether they are continuous or interrupted. It is also a help to indicate the tones of the various areas, but blank spaces of tone or colour are not as helpful as areas built up from lines or marks of texture.

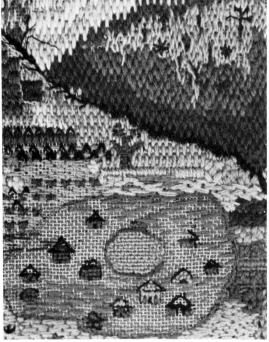

Some ways of filling a space

(1) An area of a different fabric (or the same fabric placed at a different angle), a padded shape or a hole.

(2) Repetition of lines of the same or

different thicknesses across the space (figure 7). These could be couched threads or lines of stitches, or another treatment such as pleating.

(3) A continuous line which can be a scribble, a looped or overlapping line, or a line following a shape or pattern such as a spiral.

(4) Lines radiating out from a point within the space.

(5) Lines crossing over each other at different angles. These can fill the space or go around the edge of it.

(6) A repetition or similar shapes of the same or different sizes. These could be a particular stitch, circles or other geometric shapes, or shapes such as letters or flowers.

(7) A repetition of patterns such as hatching, scrolls or patterns built up from combinations of stitches.

(8) Irregular texture, which could be a combination of two or more of the above suggestions such as lines and circles (straight stitches, looped threads and eyelets).

Some ways of getting from one place to another

(1) A single line. This can be wide or narrow; straight, curved or wavy; coiled or knotted. The line may be made by stitching or some other treatment, or it can be a join.

(2) A repetition of lines going in the direction of the line to be marked. These can be continuous or interrupted and more or less parallel to each other (figure 8).

(3) A repetition of lines or stitches at an opposing angle to the direction of travel. The angle may be varied and the lines can cross each other.

(4) A repetition of shapes, stitches or patterns. These can be isolated stitches such as spider's webs, geometric shapes, or some other shapes like a row of trees or buildings.

(5) A combination of any of the above suggestions.

Usually a piece of work has lines and spaces in it, and suggestions from both groups might be used together.

Ways of making lines and textures other than by using standard stitch forms are covered in more detail later, as are ways of translating textures observed on natural and man-made surfaces (figures 9 and 10) into threads and fabrics (figure 11).

Experiments can be tried at any time when an idea occurs and can be kept to use when needed. The layout of the sampler should be more interesting than just rows or blobs of stitches scattered about the fabric. It need only be very simple to start with; for example lines radiating from the centre can be used, or a curved shape such as the letter 'C' can be followed. Ideas for the design of the sampler can often come from the object one is looking at for inspiration for textural treatments (figures 12 and 13), still more is learnt from placing stitches or textures next to other textures and by making them relate to each other.

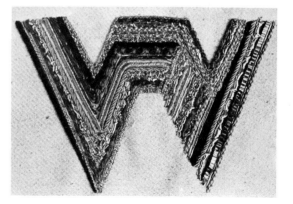

7 A repetition of lines used to fill a space; Russia braid, cords, Jap gold and passing with rust and black wool on cream silk

8 Lines travelling from one place to another, continuous and interrupted; this was worked in pearl purl

9 A Letraset texture much enlarged which suggests knots and ruched threads

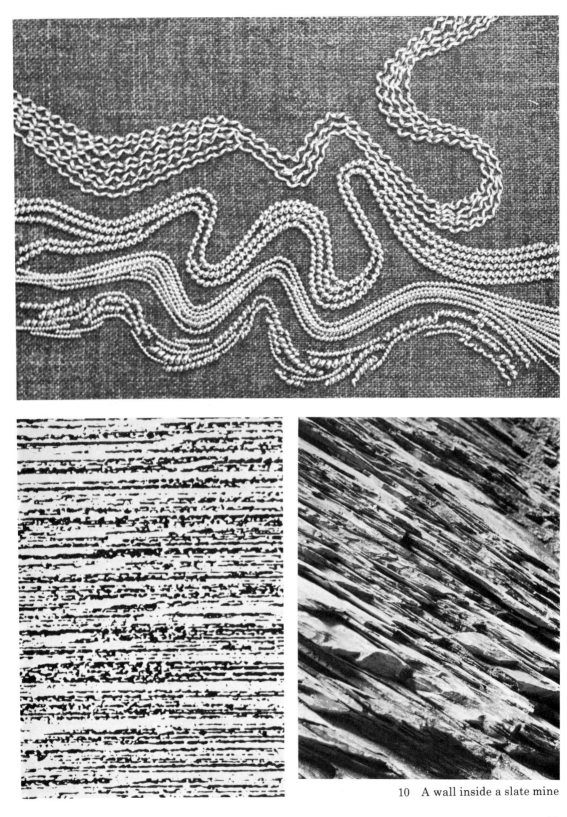

10   A wall inside a slate mine

11 A detail of 'Reflections' by Valerie
Campbell-Harding. The canvas work
background was built up with short lengths of
stitches which were worked almost at random
over the whole area and which then were
gradually filled in. Tent, satin, back, straight
and Portuguese knotted stem stitches in wools
and mohair, with coloured cocktail sticks, were
used

12 A pile of wood planks in a builder's yard

13 A simple design for a sampler. The dark
lines were worked first in satin and long-
armed cross, and the fillings were worked
afterwards. Chained cross, looped half-cross,
plaited square and other canvas stitches were
used

15

SOVRCES OF IDEAS

Closely observed detail, often very enlarged, can suggest ways of using materials (figure 14). It is not necessary only to look at the rich and rare. Many very ordinary things, both natural and man-made, would repay a closer look. Use a magnifying glass sometimes, take photographs and keep a sketchbook; but take the camera and sketchbook with you wherever you go, and do not be afraid to photograph or draw in public. The sketches need not be expert and may need notes to supplement them, but if you do not make a habit of collecting ideas you will have nothing to base an experiment on. Texture is difficult to draw, and often marks can only suggest it, but these marks can be made with different media such as ink or charcoal, pen or brush.

For ideas to translate into experiments let us consider the following: natural texture; man-made textures; accidental and experimental happenings.

NATURAL TEXTURE

This is the largest source of ideas, and different things appeal to different people (figures 15, 16, 17 and 18). Look at growth patterns, water movements, frost, shells, stems and leaves, fungus, wasps' nests, seed heads, fruit or vegetables. A piece of wood or stone, if looked at closely, can be seen to have small marks and interruptions which could be emphasized and enlarged. Microscope slides of many things show patterns and shapes that suggest different textural treatments.

MAN-MADE TEXTURES

Many household objects made of glass, metal, pottery or plastic will give ideas (figures 19, 20 and 21). Kitchen tools,

14   A detail of a clump of fungus growing at the base of a tree

17

15 A lettuce cut in half suggests ways either of manipulating fabric or of looping or swirling threads. The plain areas are a needed relief to the intricate folds

16 Backlighting on the ridges of a beach gives rather hard edges to the shapes, in contrast with the rounded stones

17 A Banyan (fig) tree in Malta. Rouleaux of varying thicknesses, plaits or wrapped threads could be intertwined to give this effect on top of stuffed areas

food, jewellery, rugs, wallpaper or corrugated paper, fabrics, packaging materials and also things from further afield like thatched roofs, machinery, scaffolding and piles of building material deserve attention.

ACCIDENTAL AND EXPERIMENTAL HAPPENINGS

From time to time it is worth playing with things like paint, glue or wax just to see what happens (figures 22, 23, 24, 25 and 26). Paper can be rolled, folded, torn, cut or crumpled and then it can be glued to a card to hold it in place. Paint or ink can be blown, splashed or combed; it can have things pressed into it or can be dropped into water (figures 27 and 28). Glue can be dribbled; it can be pulled into long threads; or it can be mixed with paint and swirled. Many things can be dipped into ink and then can be printed onto paper or straight onto the fabric. Rubbings are easy to do using greaseproof paper and wax crayon; when they are photo-

graphed and greatly enlarged, they can look totally unlike the original surface. String, seeds, paper clips, wood shavings, straws and many other objects can be glued to paper to make textures which can be interpreted in threads and fabrics.

Corrosion, rotting and weathering produce many fascinating things such as skeletonized leaves and badly rusted metal which are more interesting than the original surface (figure 29).

Touch things if possible, as this adds to the knowledge of the texture (figures 30 and 31). Open things up to see what is inside, or break them in half. Sometimes curiosity is a virtue.

A collection of small objects should be kept such as bones, fossils, stones, twisted metal shapes, roots and branches, dried flowers or a piece of crazed glass. These can be looked at when ideas run short. It is a good idea to keep a scrapbook with illustrations of textures gathered from papers and magazines and to buy postcards from

museums.

The subject of a design may suggest a technique, such as a small piece of bark leading to the treatment of a whole clump of trees, but often ideas for texture come from sources that are totally unconnected with that particular subject. It is very productive to take one object such as half a cabbage and to interpret it in different ways (another example is given in figures 32 and 33). Take a photograph; draw it with a pen; print it with ink onto paper; interpret it with torn tissue paper and glue; take a rubbing of it; or lay a bundle of threads on a piece of paper and make swirls in it with your finger until it resembles the growth formation of the cabbage. Some of these experiments could be carried out in padding or stuffing, cut work or stitchery worked on layers of Perspex.

All this does take time, but it is immensely enjoyable and rewarding. It is often difficult not to use ideas based on other people's work, and if one does not build up a reference in this way there is nothing to fall back on when a new treatment is wanted; the tendency then is to see what someone else has done and to do the same.

18   A field of straw. This suggests straight stitches, tufting or frayed fabric

19   The base of a glass tumbler which is covered with irregular nobs

(black and white photos, p. 21)
20   *opposite* This embossed plastic is sold as a wall tile. A much better use for it is as an idea for quilting or stuffing; it could also be cut up, and the small pieces could be incorporated into an embroidery

21   A close-up of a piece of Medina glass

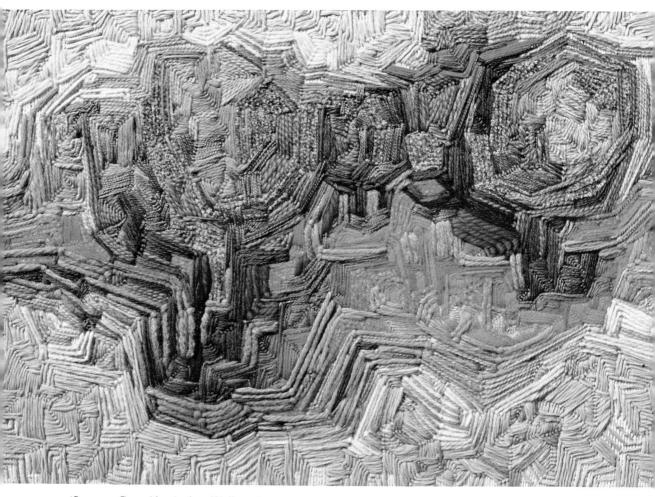

'Summer Grove' by Audrey Walker. The whole
panel is worked in fly stitch in wools, chenille,
perle and strandard cotton. There is great variety
in the thickness of the threads, and the size and
varying angles of the stitches. In some places
the background is allowed to show through.

-Colour plate facing p. 20-

'Reflections' by Valerie Campbell-Harding.
Canvaswork panel based on reflections on water
with an area of turbulence caused by the
passing of a boat.

-Colour plate facing p. 44-

'Waterfall' by Jane Clarke. Velvet, suede,
chiffon and net are used on hessian.

-Colour plate facing p. 45-

'Grotto' by Margaret Barr. A panel worked in
orthodox canvas stitches used in an imaginative
way that gives an impression of depth.

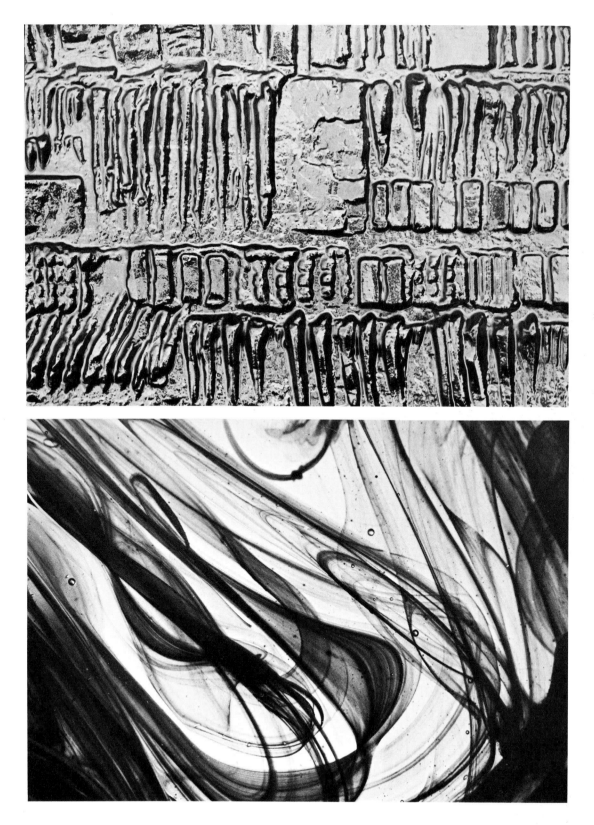

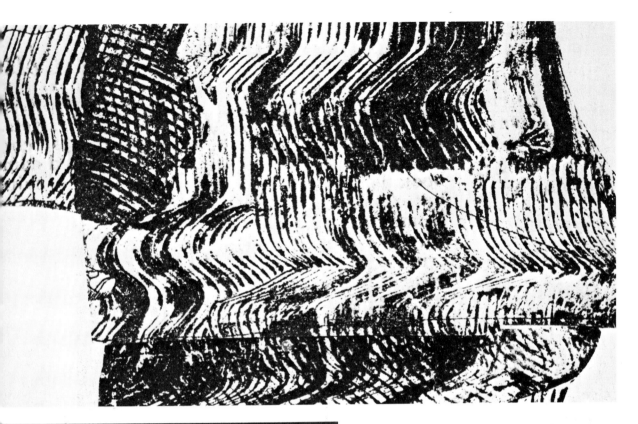

22   Combed ink patterns photographed from a newspaper illustration

23   Wet tissue was placed on a piece of card, and then it was moved about until a pleasing result was obtained. The idea was based on a fast-flowing river with many large rocks in it

24   Playing with paper is a good starting point for experimenting with fabrics. Paper was torn and rolled into cylinders. Metallic foil was moulded over pencil ends, and small pieces of tissue paper were scrunched up to make an irregular texture in the background

25   Thick oil paint was dabbed onto card with a knife and the beads stuck into it before it hardened. An experiment like this is a design as well as a rich texture, and it could easily be adapted for embroidery

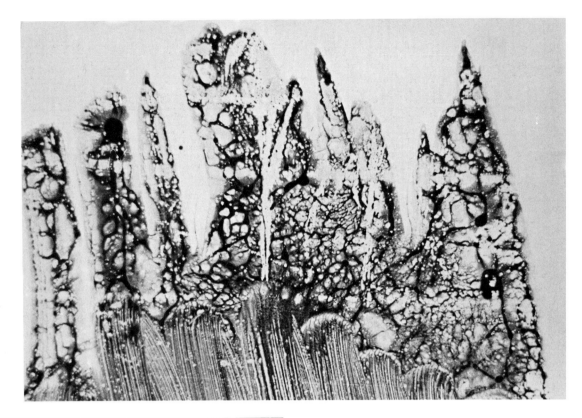

26 Ink on an enamel dish. The dish was dampened first so that the paint did not stick to it and so that it separated into amorphous patterns. The streaks at the bottom were made by rubbing with a finger

27 Paint poured onto a turntable which spins very quickly. This was done at Battersea Fun Fair but could be attempted on an old gramophone. This suggests many pieces of transparent fabrics overlapping each other with some holes cut in places and stitchery on top (Jonathan Harding)

28 Swirls of paint on a shop window. Smooth couching in metal threads would give emphasis to the change of direction

29 Rotted wood and rusty nails (Jonathan Harding)

25

30 A piece of charred wood with interesting variations on a basic shape and also surface texture which suggests stitch treatments. Thread could be wrapped over fabric-covered card shapes with stitchery worked on top

31 Sticky-backed plastic which had been used to cover an old tray. Heat and old age has caused the plastic to wrinkle

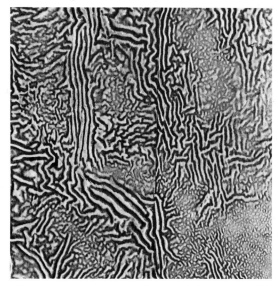

32 A photograph of a fossil which suggests a patchwork of fabrics with stuffing or padding and beads.

33   A drawing of the same fossil which shows an entirely different approach and which could be carried out in stitchery alone (Sarah Harding)

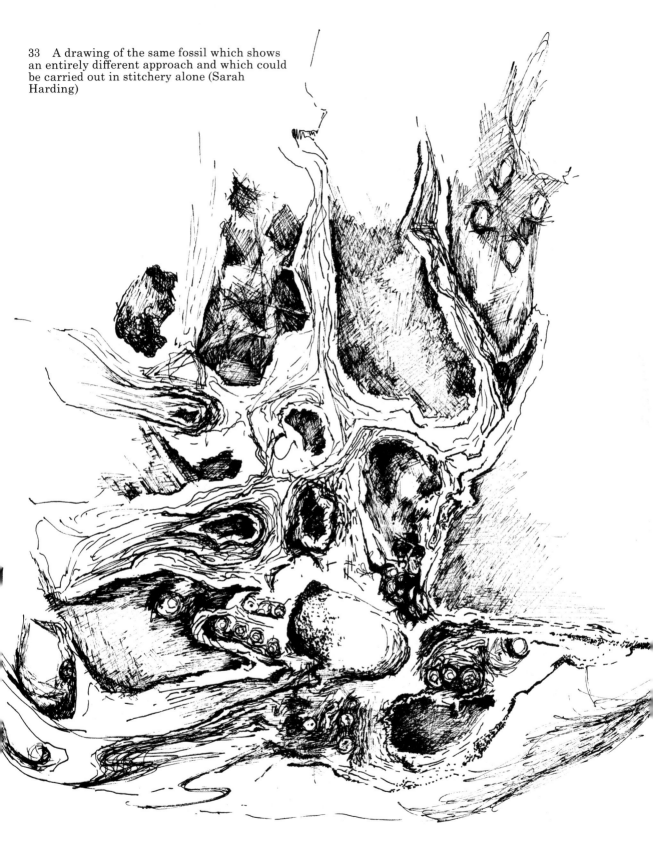

THREAD

Threads are the basis of all embroidery and can make marks, patterns or texture. They can be thick or thin, smooth or hairy, twisted or stranded. They can be made of almost anything – cotton, wool, silk, jute, nylon, fibre glass, cellophane or metal – and can be even along the length of the thread or can have knots, lumps or knobbles in them. Threads can be pliable, limp, stiff, wiry or springy. Each type reacts differently and must be experimented with to discover its particular characteristics, assets and disadvantages. There are many embroidery threads available and also those used mainly for weaving, knitting, crochet or macramé. Many other objects can be used such as thongs, pipe cleaners, shoelaces, fishing lines, wire, piping cord, string, threads pulled from woven fabrics or strips of fabric.

The same colour in different threads can look quite different, and use can be made of this to give a rich and varied tone value to one piece of work. Altering the direction of the threads or stitches also changes the tone; this can add emphasis to certain areas of the design or it can subdue them. This applies particularly to shiny or metallic threads.

Threads can be used with sewing or knitting needles, crochet or rug hooks, shuttles or one's fingers; the correct tool should be chosen that gives the result required at the time.

There are two main ways of making texture with threads. One is to make stitches with them, and the other is to manipulate them either before or during the sewing process. Some threads can be split or untwisted and can be used while opened out; they can be divided and then the parts can be used separately. Some can be doubled up or used in groups or bundles. Threads can be knotted or frayed; or they can be sewn closely in some places and the strands allowed to escape in others. Threads can be looped, twisted (figures 34 and 35) or braided to add texture when the untreated thread may be too thin or uninteresting. Some threads, such as Anchor soft or perle, can be ruched. If one of the strands (or the core) is pulled and the

34   The underside of a rush chair seat which suggests twisting threads

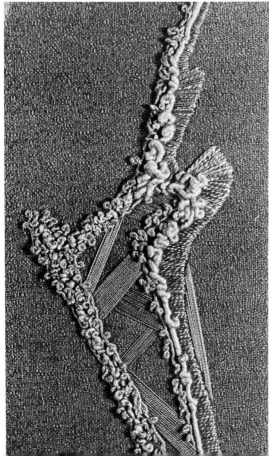

35   A thread was twisted tightly enough to make it corkscrew back onto itself. If more than one colour or type of thread is twisted together, a wide range of shades and textures can be made

36 A sampler based on a drawing of a shoulder muscle. The rounded part was achieved by padding with six layers of felt. The result bears no resemblance at all to the original idea, but this does not matter. Ruched and whipped threads on a printed fabric were used

37 Unexpected sources of inspiration are everywhere. These noodles suggest bundles of threads

rest gently eased back the result is an irregular corkscrew around the straight pulled thread. This is couched, and the ends are taken through the back afterwards.

Threads and stitches can be used flat or over padding or across a hole (figure 36). They can be worked on top of an opaque material or under a transparent one or over a piece of mirror or foil to reflect them. They can be worked through a fabric; they can be semi-detached by working through a foundation of stitches; they can be worked in the hand not using a fabric at all, for example they can be bundled or rolled (figures 37 and 38).

Threads can be wound or wrapped around other threads or objects (figure 39). They can be taken through holes in stones or shells or through straws or tubes. If these tubes are transparent they will protect the threads while displaying them. Short lengths of threads can be tied in bundles and attached, and this could be a use for the cut ends which are usually discarded.

All this playing with threads suggests possibilities for their use and helps to free one from acquired inhibitions. Some of these suggestions are not very practical, but they could be used on a panel or with some form of protection.

MASSED THREADS

A massed effect with threads or stitches can be used to cover the whole area or background as in canvas work, or it can be used in places to contrast with thinner embroidery or plain fabric. It can give areas of texture, or it can fill in a hard-edged shape in a design. Massed stitchery can give richness and depth, but care must be taken to avoid a congested look which can so easily happen.

Embroidery on canvas has great scope for solid textural effects as thick threads or ribbons will pull through easily and the background need not be totally covered. It could be left plain or painted if it looks too bare. Some ideas for stitching on canvas can be gleaned from looking at woven fabrics

38 Rolls of threads are held in place with nylon stocking

39 Pieces of card have threads wrapped around them before being stuck to the background; the ends are glued at the back. The threads could be closer together or cross over each other

(figures 40 and 41). A tweed can be imitated incorporating the loops, knobs or weave variations and patterns that are in the piece of fabric. Underside couching is not much used now, but it works well on canvas or hessian, and threads can be used for this which are too delicate or too knobbly to sew with.

Laidwork consists of long threads laid close together across the shape to be filled (figure 42). If the embroidery is stretched tightly while being worked, and also when it is finally mounted, it is not necessary to hold down these long threads unless additional texture is wanted or padding is used under them. The whole shape can be covered or gaps can be left in places; these are as important as the laid areas in the final result.

Various ways of adding more texture and

40 Fabrics can give ideas for textural treatments. This tweed was imitated on canvas

securing the laid threads at the same time can be tried. The knobs and ridges on shells suggest detached stitches, spider's webs or ridges of stitching such as whipped chain, all worked on top of laid threads. Detached buttonhole rings or slices of polythene tubing can be placed on top and held down with long threads leading from them. Fly, herringbone or cretan stitch will hold laid threads, and also some composite stitches such as raised chain band.

Goldwork is, perhaps, at its most beautiful when given rich treatment, even if only in parts of a design as a contrast to the open areas. It is a mistake to consider any method

of embroidery as being in a separate pigeon-hole from the others, and many things attempted with coloured threads can also be tried with metal ones (figure 43). The contrast between rough and smooth is particularly noticeable when using metal threads.

Flat close couching of gold threads is a basic technique which should be mastered as it is the foundation of this type of embroidery, but the traditional method of working this can be varied (figures 44 and 45). One way is by couching more threads on top of couched threads to make ridges, either parallel to the original lines, or across them, making shapes or patterns. This can solve the difficulty of where to take the ends through to the back without interrupting the flow; therefore instead of taking them through bring the threads up on top of the already couched ones in places where the line or shape gets thinner and then down onto the fabric again where the line gets wider. A thread could also be looped, coiled

41 Corded rayon imitated by couching threads over string

or twisted with the next one to break the evenness of the couching.

There is a great variety of gold threads available, but a dearth of copper ones; so even more ingenuity must be used in making the most of what we have. A certain thick copper cord can be untwisted to make three smaller ones; each of these when again untwisted will be found to consist of many fine copper threads wound around a core, and these can be used together or separately. Copper wires can be pulled from the inside of electric flex, although this is a struggle without an electrician's wire-stripper. A copper scouring pad will unravel; it is stiff enough to hold in a shape and could be coiled or twisted. Various thicknesses of copper wire are sold for making jewellery, but are very stiff; copper-coloured ties for freezer bags are more pliable.

COILED AND LOOPED THREADS

Apart from making looped stitches, threads can be looped or coiled and then couched (figure 47). Most threads will do this easily and so will groups of threads; they can be held in place with tiny stitches that hardly show or can have one long stitch going from the centre of one coil to the centre of the next. Coils can also be raised off the fabric and this is easier if they are made by winding the thread around a knitting needle between each stitch. Each loop should be held with a small back stitch.

Satin stitch worked loosely over a rod or stick will remain as small loops when the rod is removed if the fabric is closely woven. Do not work too long a length at a time as it will be too difficult to remove the rod.

Threads can be wrapped around the fingers or a piece of card, as if you were making a simple tassel, and then they can be taken off and held together in the middle to prevent them unwinding. The skein can then be secured to the fabric with satin stitches covering the centre part of it and with loops showing at either end. The skein can also be attached by just one or two stitches holding it at one point only so that it hangs freely, and parts of it may be wrapped or button-holed.

Loops can also be made in a piece of knitting or crochet by winding the threads round one or two fingers between each stitch.

CROCHET AND KNITTING

Shapes of crochet or knitting can be applied to a fabric either flat or over padding or gathered or distorted (figures 48 and 49). Work these pieces on fairly large needles.

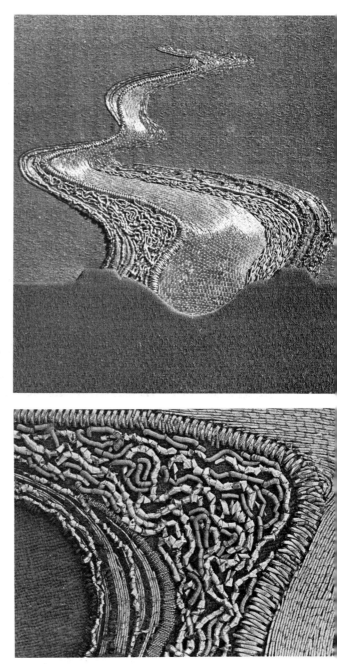

42   Laid threads over card shapes placed between the fabric and the backing. The change of direction of the threads alters the tone

43   Ruched Jap gold, cut purl and pieces cut from a military fringe were coiled and sewn to the fabric ground. The coils are rather fragile and would need protection. The idea for this came from looking at wood shavings on the floor

44   'River Dam' by Valerie Campbell-Harding. The smooth couched gold is the original river, and the textured areas at the sides are where the river has overflowed its banks onto the grass and weeds

45   A close-up of the edge showing the texture of ruched Jap gold, cut purl attached in hoops and flat gold zigzagged over string

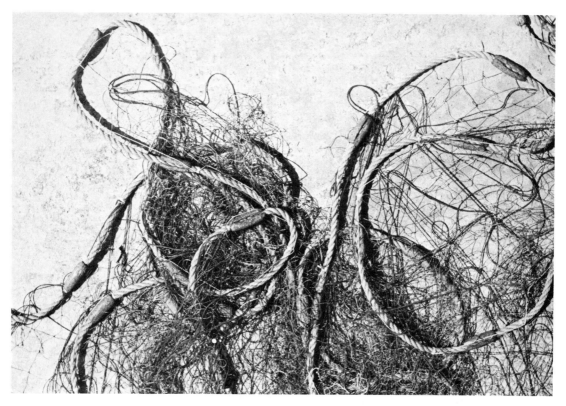

46 Fishing nets

47 Gold purl does not necessarily have to be cut into short lengths and sewn on like beads. When looped as it is here the stitches do show but are not too objectionable

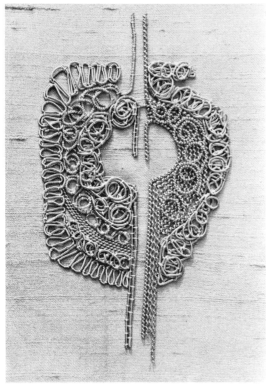

48 'Lichen' by Jan Messent. Areas of flat stitching on canvas with applied crochet were used. Cups in double crochet, lengths of fur stitch and some wavy crochet shapes were made by hand and then were attached

Holes and dropped stitches can give variation and so can stitches worked over the top.

Tubular knitting, which is worked on four nails in the top of a cotton reel, can be used as a thread and could be padded with string. More nails can be hammered into a wooden curtain ring to make a larger tube.

Moulds can be covered in crochet, and double crochet is probably the best stitch for this. Save objects such as bottle tops, parts of old toys, polystyrene balls or old plastic bangles, and cover them.

A crochet stitch, which will make spiral 'acorn' shapes that can dangle or which will untwist and be applied as an overall texture, is made by first working a long chain, then by working three trebles into the fourth chain back from the hook and three trebles into every following chain.

WEAVING

Needleweaving can be worked on a fabric from which some threads have been withdrawn in one direction, or it can be worked on threads which are laid over the surface in varying directions (figures 50 and 51). A frame is needed when using the second method, or the weaving can be worked on something stiff such as Perspex or an object. It is a very versatile type of embroidery and can be worked with textured threads or with other stitches between the rows of weaving. Separate pieces of weaving worked on a notched card or a bead loom can be applied; they could be twisted, rolled over padding or sewn at one edge to hang free.

KNOTTING AND BRAIDING

French knots, if worked with a stiff or metallic thread, will leave loops instead of a tight knot. Individual knots can be tied in a thick thread, or they can be cut off and sewn to a fabric leaving the short ends showing. These knots could hang in a loop with the ends tied at the back of the work, or they could hang from the bottom edge of a panel

37

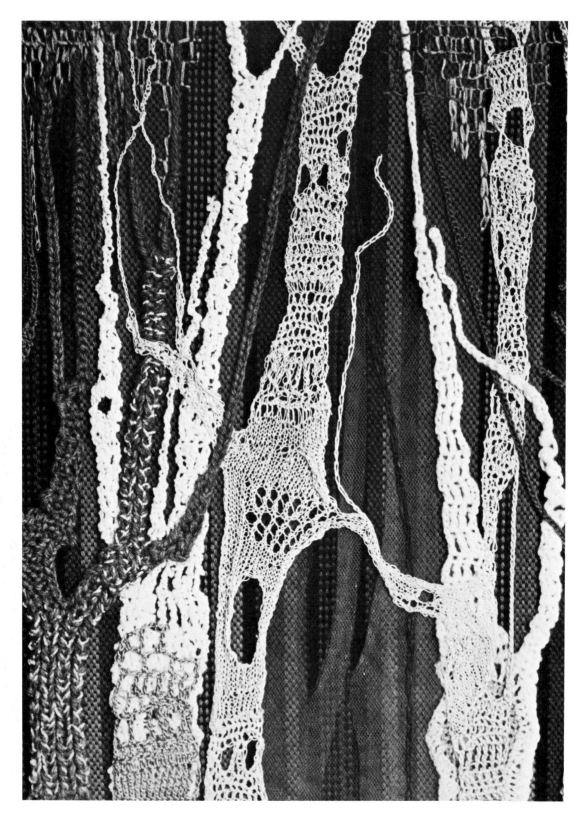

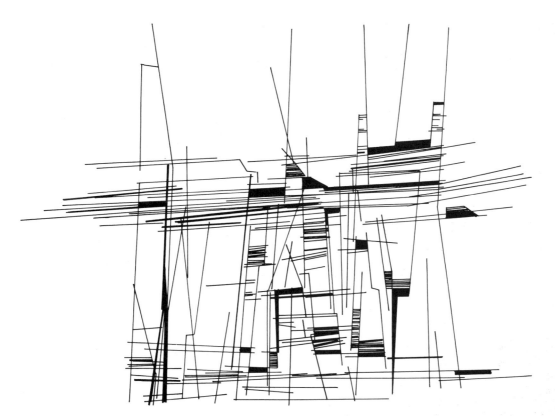

49 'Trees' by Jan Messent. Irregular knitting was applied over net and some stitching onto a tweed fabric

50 A stylized drawing of a marble cliff. A framework of straight threads could be laid, and then it could be built up on with weaving, buttonhole, raised chain band and other stitches

51 Needleweaving worked on threads laced over fabric-covered card with some knots. Lumpy weaving yarn, fine wool and raffia were used

or from the lid of a box.

Cords, braids or sennets can be attached at one end or both. These cords can be made with loops between each twist or knot to interrupt the regular pattern; they can be made with a lumpy thread or one that has been previously knotted.

Macramé will combine with embroidery and can be worked on threads brought through from the back of the work (figure 52). Rows of half-hitches produce a series of ridges, and the loose ends can be left showing. Try working macramé very loosely with gaps between the knots, or alternatively by working it with strips of fabric.

TUFTING AND HOOKING

Tufting can be made by sewing or knitting loops and then by cutting them or also by working velvet or knotted stitches. A rug hook will make a pile on a loosely woven fabric; however, knots with the ends left hanging are better either on a tighter weave or worked with back stitch leaving the top half of the stitch as a loop.

Some sewing machines have a tailor tacking foot which has a high ridge of metal in the middle over which zigzag is worked in loops. Rows of these can be worked closely packed together, and the only disadvantage is that a thick thread cannot be used nor can the length of the loop be varied. However, the same sort of thing could be attempted by hand if a small piece of card held upright was sewn over and then was moved along as the stitching progressed. This might have to be glued on the back of the fabric to keep the loops in place.

A tufted effect can also be achieved by making many small tassels and then sewing them on. One can also make wool balls as one did when a child by winding wool over two discs made of card, each with a central hole, and then cutting around the edge. A length of the wool is wrapped tightly round the centre before removing the card.

52 Looped macramé cords, looped back stitch and knots in wool, tape, russia braid, velvet thread and raffia

STITCHES

It is not necessary to learn a great number of stitches, but it is important to know some very well, to explore their possibilities and to see how the basic form can be varied. Stitches can be patternd-forming units, and they can build up to make quite complicated ones. They can indicate direction or movement; they can convey an idea; they can add emphasis or detail in certain places; they can provide a link between a strongly textured or raised area and the background (figures 53 and 54). It is therefore essential to work some samplers with stitches in many types of threads on different fabrics in order to discover which one serves the purpose best. They need not be elaborate, and a simple one like running stitch in a very thick thread might be the only treatment needed.

HOW TO VARY A STITCH

As a starting point select one stitch and try some of the following variations (figure 55).

(1) *Work the stitch in different threads.* Use thick, medium and very fine ones, and also try unusual threads and fabrics. The same stitch in one strand of cotton on organdie will look very different worked in macramé cord on hessian or wire mesh (figures 56 and 57). Aim at achieving delicacy and strength in the same stitch. Use more than one colour or thread in the needle at the same time. This works particularly well with canvas stitches. Chain stitch worked with five or six threads together will look more interesting and make a wider line.

(2) *Vary the tension of the stitch.* It can be pulled tight to rise up from the surface of the fabric or can be left loose to lie flat on it. Also vary the fabric as this affects the tension; a stitch that on one fabric is a wide line stitch can, on a very loosely woven fabric, turn into a stitch which pulls the fabric threads together and itself becomes much narrower. This variation of tension must be deliberate as otherwise the result will look like poor technique.

(3) *Vary the size of the stitch.* Most stitches can be worked very small or very large – two

53 'Path to the Watergarden' by Jan Beaney. Ruffled chiffon, net, ribbon and lurex were used on an evenweave background. This panel shows how effective straight stitches can be. The french and bullion knots add contrast

54 A detail of 'Path to the Watergarden'

or more sizes of a single stitch can be used together to fill spaces with texture or to build up into decorative patterns or borders (figure 58).

(4) *Vary the spacing and the regularity of the stitch.* Aim for rhythm rather than for precision. Some people find this easier to do when stitching on a slight curve than on a straight line.

(5) *Alter the proportion* of the whole or part of the stitch. It can be long and thin or short and fat. One side can be made larger than the other, such as one leg of fly or twisted chain (figure 59). The final loops of knotted cable chain or pekinese can be different lengths and can be very long. Buttonhole or open chain can be a narrow or a very wide band, or a gradual change from one to the other.

(6) *Work the stitch at different angles and directions* (the design could be taken from figure 60). All the stitches could lean one way, they could cross over each other or they could make a fan shape. Some stitches, such

as buttonhole, can be worked in alternate directions along a line instead of all facing the same way.

(7) *Work the stitch double* or part of it double. Each stage of some stitches such as wheatear or pekinese can be repeated before moving on to the next stage. Raised chain band can be worked two or even three times on each rung of the ladder to make it more knobbly. Sometimes a large stitch such as chain or spider's web can be worked around the outside of a smaller one.

(8) *Work the stitches on top of each other.* This can be done with a thick thread over a thin one or stitches worked in one direction over threads or stitches travelling in another direction (figure 61). Knots can be worked on top of areas of stitching to break up the evenness, and a thin spiky version of a stitch such as cretan can be used over itself in many layers to give a feeling of depth.

(9) *Try a detached form of the stitch.* Many line stitches can be used in a detached form as a single shape or in short lengths. Try this with herringbone or cretan, or one of the chains.

(10) *Work only part of a stitch.* Many stitches can be made using only the first stage of them (figures 62 and 63). Try this with ladder stitch, herringbone, eyelets or Portuguese border stitch.

(11) *Try stitches as lines,* making them narrow and wide. Sometimes these lines can be interlocked with each other, and sometimes they can be whipped or threaded together to make them broader.

(12) *Try stitches as fillings,* either open or solid, or graduating from one to the other either by changing to thicker threads or by working the stitches closer together (figure 64).

(13) *Work the reverse of the stitch.* A composite stitch such as raised stem band can be worked from back to front leaving a series of ridges (figure 65). A stitch can be worked on the back of the fabric so that the wrong side shows, just as the reverse of back stitch is stem stitch. Always look at the back of your work just to see if there is

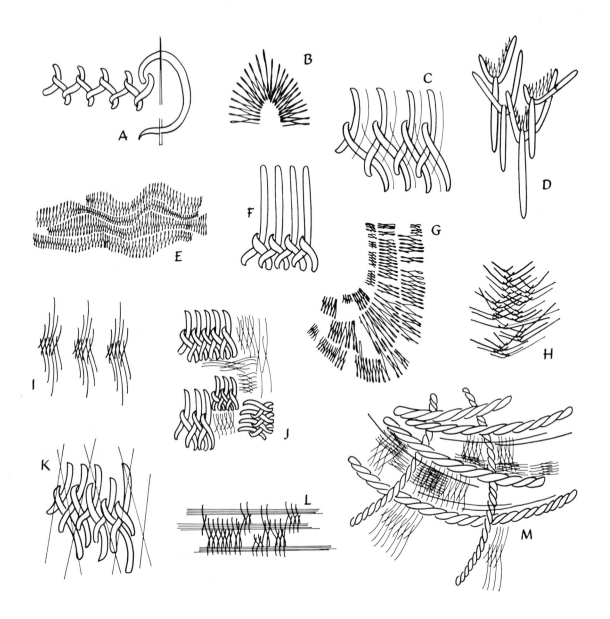

55 Variations on cretan stitch: A, the basic
form; B, used to fill a shape; C, a thin thread is
used over a thick one; D, cretan combined with
fly stitch; E, the size is varied to give a
rhythmical effect; F, the proportion is altered
by taking a much larger stitch through the
fabric on one side; G, used as a block pattern;
H, by altering the angle of the needle as it picks
up the fabric cretan stitch is turned into feather
stitch; I, used as a repeating spot pattern;
J, different sizes and weights of the stitch are
combined to make a textural area; K, cretan
combined with herringbone; L, used to hold
groups of threads; M, cretan and whipped
backstitch worked in different directions

(black and white photo, p. 45)

56 Buttonholed loops, which are usually
worked in fine thread on dresses, make an
interesting texture when worked in double rug
wool. Some of the loops have picots or extra
loops worked on them

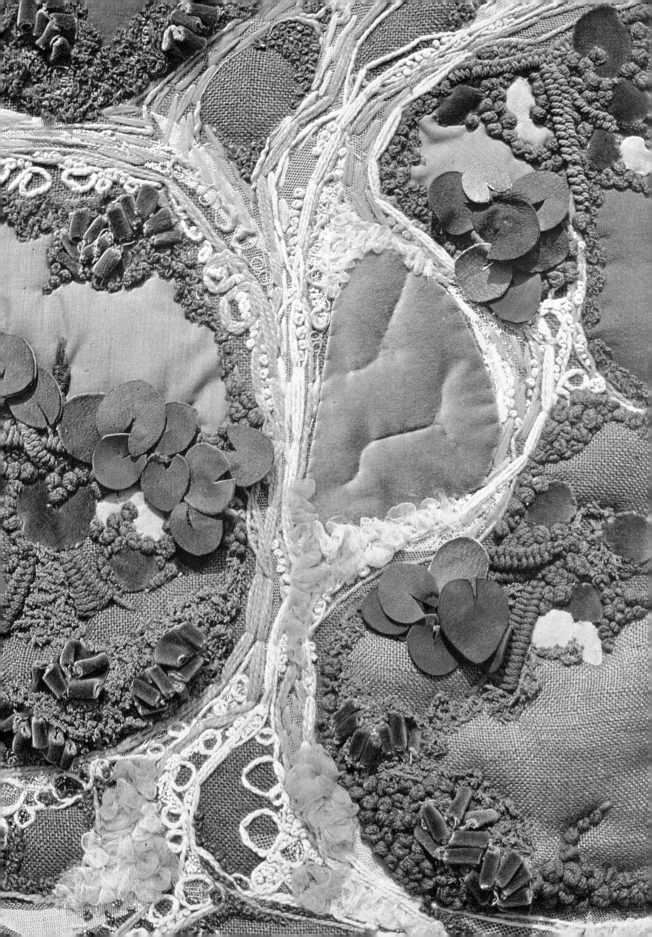

an idea there.

(14) *Use stitches to hold things down.* These can be other stitches which might be a bit loose and therefore prone to snagging or solely for their decorative effect. Stitches will also hold long threads, ribbon or braid and also objects such as beads, rods or sticks.

(15) *Use different stitches with other,* or more than one, versions of the same stitch, to build up patterns. These can be borders, circles or squares. Some stitches that fit

well together are fly, chain, herringbone, sheaf, knots and straight stitches. When you have done one that you like, try it again using threads of different weights, so that a border with a heavy bottom edge could change into one with a heavy band running along the middle. If ideas are lacking for these patterns study patterns on other surfaces like shells, feathers, snowflakes or a field of barley (figure 66).

These are only suggestions and they will

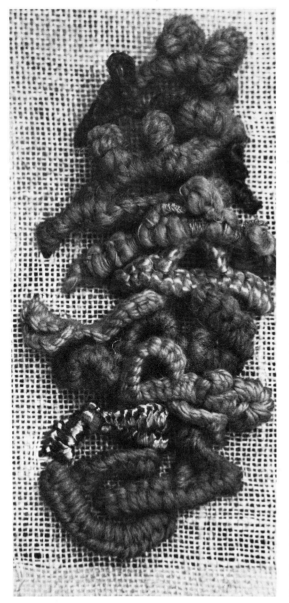

57 French knots worked in tape, raffia, string and strips of builders' scrim on hessian. The straight stitches help to integrate the heavy embroidery with the background *(above)*

58 A detail of 'Summer Grove' by Audrey Walker. This illustrates just how rich a texture a single stitch can make *(below)*

45

not all work with every stitch. As work progresses further ideas will begin to flow freely as they do when one is actually using the threads and fabrics. Aim for contrast in the stitching (figure 67) and the juxtaposition of thin and thick, matt and shiny, smooth and textured. A plain area can have a broken one near it, and large stitches near small ones, to give vitality.

When some of these have been tried and stitches become familiar use the stitches to carry out your impressions of a subject such as water, shadows, wind in a field of wheat or a piece of rock (figure 68). Study the subject closely, either draw or photograph it and then work it in stitchery; alternatively work the stitchery while looking at the object

without any intermediate stage (figure 69).

It is not a good idea to mix too many different stitches in one piece of work as this looks busy. It is far better to use very few, or even only one, with variations of it together – this really makes it work for you. There is no end to the possibilities of stitch variation although some are more adaptable than others. The only limitations are whether a particular yarn can be pulled through a certain fabric or whether it must lie on top of it, and also the purpose for which the stitchery is intended.

59   A knitted fabric which suggests ways of altering the size or proportion of chain or fly stitch

60 This photograph of leaves shows a variety
in size and direction that can be imitated in
stitchery

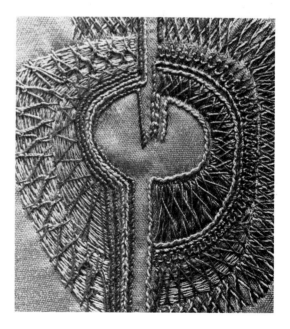

61 This bud is worked in variations of
herringbone stitch. The stitch is worked double,
with one layer worked over another; over an
area of stem stitch; and it is whipped and
knotted

62 A decayed prickly pear leaf

63 A sampler based on figure 62 worked in ladder stitch. In parts only half the stitch is used, and it has been worked on top of itself to add density

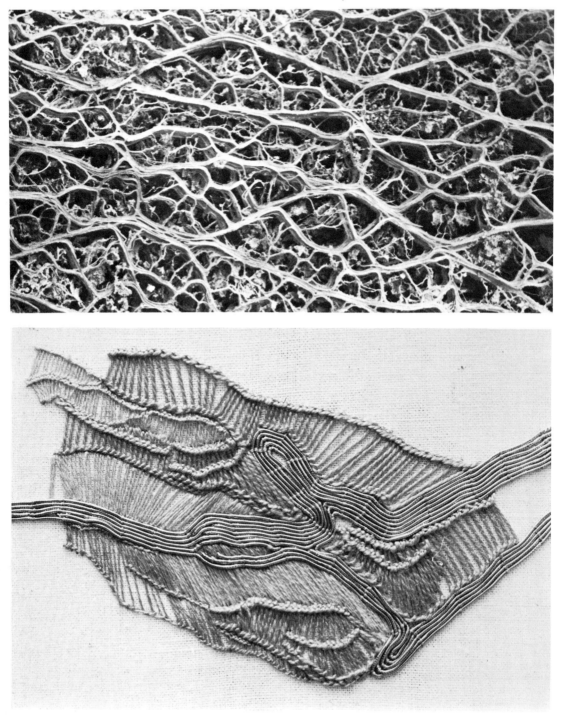

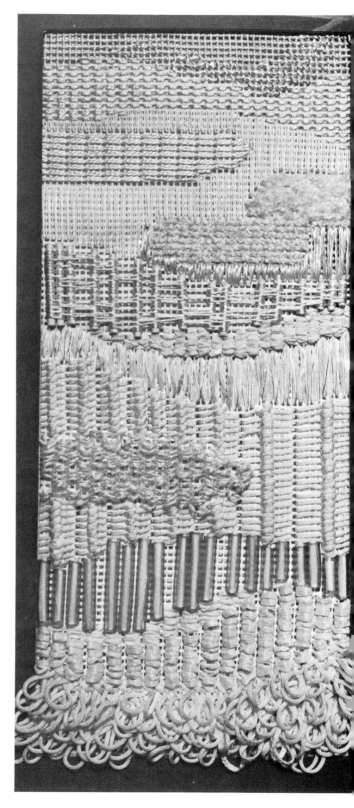

64 A white sampler of stitches used as fillings worked on a very coarse fabric. Starting at the top the stitches are as follows: Russian drawn ground in silk thrums and raffia; back stitch in perle; detached long chain stitches in crochet cotton; couching in perle; underside couching in poodle wool; back stitches in chenille; chain stitches in raffia; straight and satin stitches in silk thrums over paper lolly sticks; double back stitches in ribbon; straight stitches with raffia, perle and weaving thread together in the needle; whipped buttonhole in macramé cord; satin stitch worked over a knitting needle in a weaving thread; polythene tubes, with strips of plastic in them; back stitch in tape; satin stitch over a knitting needle in raffia; velvet stitch in macramé cord

65   Variations of spiders' webs including
working a part of the web. These were achieved
by working it round and over objects, by
altering the shape, by working the ridges as
separate bars, by adding extra ridges in places,
by adding other stitches and by working it in
reverse

66   This photograph of barley relates to
stitchery in the way the shapes of the grain
contrast with the long straight hairs and the
smooth stems

67   A simple exercise which shows the
effectiveness of contrast in the thickness of
the thread

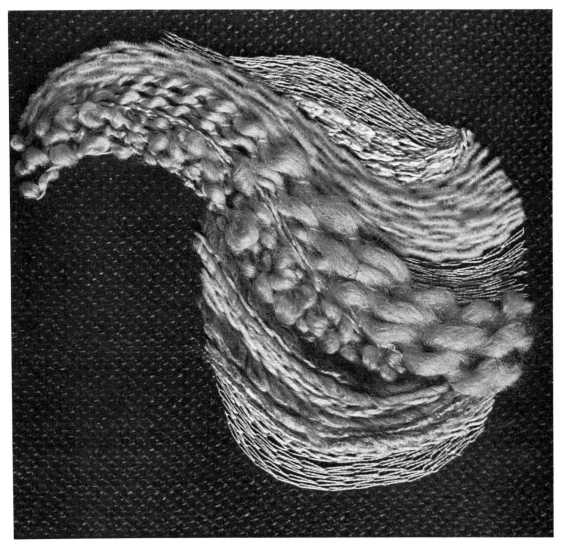

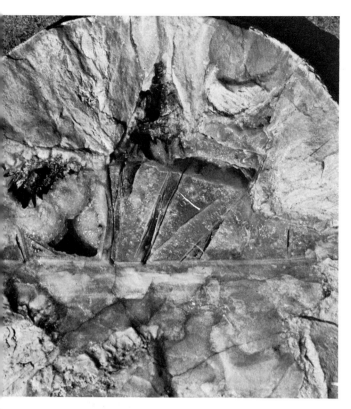

68 A slice of Australian agate known as 'thunderegg'. This could be used as a design for experimental stitchery as tone and direction are clearly indicated. If a piece of tracing paper is placed over the top, the main shapes are outlined and the holes are marked, the pattern could be transferred onto a fabric with tacking stitches. Then stitchery could be worked while continually referring to the photograph

69 A detail of a panel by Jan Messent based on a 'thunderegg'. A piece of 16s canvas was embroidered and then was applied over padding onto embroidered 10s canvas, with the edges frayed out and left showing

FABRIC

Too often fabrics are used only to provide a background or an area of colour or only for their existing textural qualities. This is a pity when so much more can be done with them. Experiments should be tried with small unwanted pieces of fabric before that fabric is finally used; these pieces can be played with to see what each will do happily, whether it will pleat, fold, fray and so on (figures 70 and 71). Textures can be produced with fabric that can be achieved in no other way, sometimes used by itself and sometimes combined with stitching. The thickness and springiness of a material influences what can be attempted with it, and it should not be forced into unsuitable methods as the results will never look right. Sometimes the reverse of a fabric can be used as well as the right side, and sometimes threads can be unravelled from a fabric to put back on top. Unusual fabrics such as garden net, wire gauze, polythene, tinfoil or gauze bandage can be used in the right place. If, like foil, they are too fragile to use by themselves they can be backed with iron-on Vilene and can then be sewn through perfectly well. perfectly well.

A collection of a wide variety of fabrics, even quite small pieces, can spark off ideas for different ways of using them. Try to have as many different weights, colours and textures as possible, as it is surprising how often one cannot find just the right piece.

APPLYING FABRICS

Applying a piece of fabric is one way of giving a change of texture, and usually the grain of the applied piece must correspond to that of the background fabric (figure 72). The applied shape can be hemmed or slip-stitched if the edges are turned under; it can be sewn by machine with two or three rows of straight stitching or a row of zigzag if they are not. The edges can be held with running stitches or embroidery stitches; they can be left untreated or can be deliberately frayed. If the work is on a frame loosen it slightly before applying pieces on

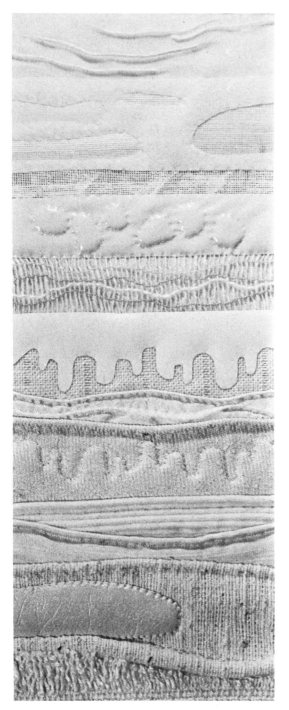

70 A sampler made to test the handling qualities of different fabrics using organdie, Vilene, tinfoil, sheer curtain fabric, PVC, gauze, linen, Thai silk, corduroy and thick tweed. The idea for the layout came from a microscope slide of human tissue

to it as they will pucker otherwise. Various ways of altering the texture of the shapes to be applied can be worked before attaching them, or they can be padded.

CUTTING

Holes or slits can be cut in a fabric to show another fabric, or stitching, underneath (figures 73 and 75). A design could be taken from figure 74. This can be done in more than one layer as in the work done by the Cuna Indians where several layers of fine cotton are cut and hemmed to the next layer, the cut-out shapes getting progressively smaller so that all the layers are showing.

If cuts are made outwards from a central point the loose pieces can be turned back, and each point can be secured with a stitch. If the fabric is turned under rather than over a piece of string or other padding can be placed in the roll to stop it being flattened.

Pieces that have been cut out can sometimes be put back somewhere else, and if at a different angle the tone may change. Circles can be punched from leather or felt with a leather punch; however, these are often too small to sew on, and they must be stuck or sewn over. A bead or stitch in the centre would secure them.

FRAYING

Some materials can be torn rather than cut, or they can have the edges frayed out to give a softer line (figure 76 could be used as a basis for the design). This can be combined with other ways of using fabrics such as folding, and the different edge should be made a feature of, in case it is thought to be due to poor workmanship. If very long threads are left after the fraying they can be used to integrate two areas by giving a third connecting colour or tone. These threads can be whipped, woven, looped or knotted, provided that they are long enough. They can also be used to indicate direction and can be raised off the ground to leave shadows.

71 Organdie, placed on the bias to avoid puckering, was laid over very shiny gold PVC, in order to subdue the glitter, and over string and felt padding to hold them in place while allowing the colour to show

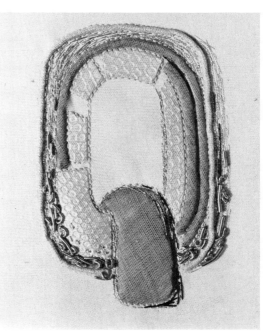

72 An unfinished panel of an ichthyosaurus skeleton. Free patchwork shapes in leather, silk and cotton were applied to a calico backing. Some edges were turned in over Vilene before hemming them

DISTORTIONS

Some loosely woven fabrics can be pulled or stretched making interesting distortions of the weave. Some threads can be pulled aside and held with stitching, or they can be withdrawn altogether in one or both directions, the remaining threads grouped together with stitching or left as they are. When some threads have been removed the remaining fabric can again be stretched and pulled to distort it still further. If some threads are pulled out for only part of their length they can then be treated in groups or bundles by twisting, wrapping, knotting or weaving; they can also be carried over to another part of the fabric and then can be attached.

73 Holes cut in gold kid to allow other fabrics to show through. Some of the cut-out pieces were put back on top. A leather punch was used for the smallest holes at the neck

74 A piece of bark, suggesting the slitting of fabric

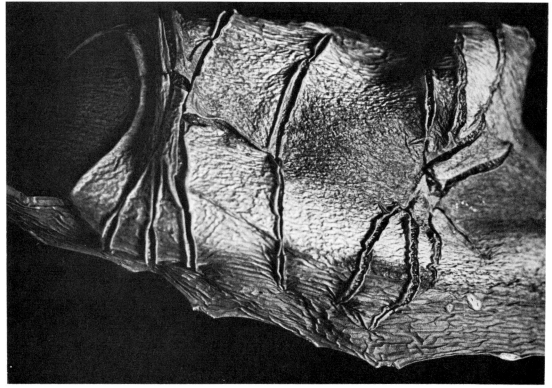

75 Part of a landscape. The leather hill at the top of the picture was slit, and strips of other colours were inserted. The stitching on each side of a slit holds a strip in place

FOLDS, PLEATS AND TUCKS

With a fairly thin fabric folds or pleats can go in more than one direction and even cross each other. The folds need not be regular, and they can be used to block out some sections of the weave or pattern and to emphasize others. This is very effective with checks or stripes, but it can also be used with some other patterns. Folds can be used to make larger patterns from a fabric with a small repeating motif or just to make texture on plain ones.

Pintucks, by hand or machine, can be worked on most fabrics or leathers or plastics, if they are not too thick. Pintucks can break up a too-shiny surface, and they can indicate direction (figures 77 and 78). If the tucks are all made in one direction they can be machined over in different and opposing directions to hold parts of the tuck to one side and parts of another.

Canvas, although not easy to manage in large pieces, can be folded or tucked to give a strong raised line or area, and it will stay stiff in use. The edges are a problem, but they could be left frayed out or covered with other fabric or stitching.

Smocking can be worked to give an irregular texture, and ideas for ways of doing this can arise from looking at bark textures or tyre marks in mud.

GATHERING AND RUCHING

Gathering can be done before a fabric is applied (the leaves in figure 79 may suggest a design), but it is often much better to ruch it while sewing it to the ground in order to control the placing of the folds (figure 80).

57

76 A palm tree which suggests frayed fabric, or strips of fabric or ribbon

77 Mushrooms

78 'Mushrooms' by Jane Lemon. The design was based on spore prints making use of the varied treatments suggested by the gills. Gold kid, grey and cream leathers, and gold and grey threads and purls on a striped fabric were used

79 Fibrous leaves at the base of a palm tree which look like wrinkled and crumpled fabrics

One edge of a piece of fabric is firmly sewn to one side of the area to be covered, and then small sections of the top fabric are pulled up with the point of the needle or are pushed to one side with a fingernail; stitches are then placed to keep the fold in place. Many fabrics look well ruched provided that they are springy and not too thick. Velvet, nylon stocking and thin leather are particularly successful, but fabrics such as silk or cotton tend to become too flat in use.

Another method is to cut a piece of cloth about twice as large as the area to be covered, to turn in a small hem all around and then to hem it into place leaving a bag of fabric standing up. Stab stitch this bag at intervals to the background.

Gathering can be worked in a spiral, wavy lines or a series of circles instead of in straight lines; this could be done on a sewing machine using shirring elastic on the bobbin.

STRIPS OF FABRIC

Cut or torn strips can be used to darn, to weave or to sew with, or to sew onto a background. They can be used flat or twisted; they can be looped, coiled, plaited or knotted depending on the effect that is wanted. When weaving strips of fabric some strips can be left as loops in the weave, or they can be twisted and knotted into place. A woven shape such as a cross or circle could be the sole decoration on a piece of work, or it could be combined with other techniques. Strips can also be made into rouleaux by folding a long strip in half lengthways, by machine stitching along the raw edges and by turning it inside out. This is easier to do if the fabric is cut on the bias and a cord, longer than the strip, is sewn to one end before it is folded. This cord is left inside the fold while it is being stitched, and it is then used to pull the rouleaux inside out.

LOOSE-EDGED ROWS

Single or multiple rows of fabric, treated in different ways, can be attached to the background in layers so that one edge is left loose, thus hiding the sewing of the row beneath it. The cone shown in figure 81 could be used as a design basis. These rows can be folded, padded, scalloped, fringed or embroidered. They can be pleated or gathered along the top edge. If the loose edge has enough threads withdrawn from it the remaining threads can be whipped, wrapped, knotted or plaited.

Separate shapes, either in rows or in a more casual arrangement, can be made and sewn on by the top edge only. These shapes should be lined or backed, and then they could be stuffed or padded; they may overlap each other to build up a three-dimensional form of patchwork.

SCRAPS

There is seldom any need to throw anything away, as even the smallest piece can be used sometimes (figure 82). Tiny scraps can be laid on fabric at varying angles, almost on top of each other, and then they can be held temporarily with a dab of glue. There is no need to worry about the direction of the grain or the raw edges. Stitching is then worked over the top of them to add interest and to secure them permanently.

POKING

Either continuous lengths or small pieces can be poked through a fairly loosely woven fabric such as hessian with a knitting needle, and secured with glue or stitching. The edges are left raw, or tape, ribbon or strips of leather can be used which need no finishing. This is very quick and easy to do, but the weave of the backing must be tight enough to hold the strips firmly.

ROLLING

Long thin triangles of plastic, leather or paper (figures 83 and 84) can be rolled, starting from the wider end and rolled towards the point, in the same way that paper beads are made by children. Short strips of fabric can be rolled and attached either lying down or up-ended. Threads, rods or tubes can be taken through the middle and can be used to attach the roll; they can also be used for their decorative effect only. If long and thin enough, rolls can be folded or bent, and they can be raised up over something else.

Many of these treatments are not easy to imagine, and they really must be tried with the fabric in the hand.

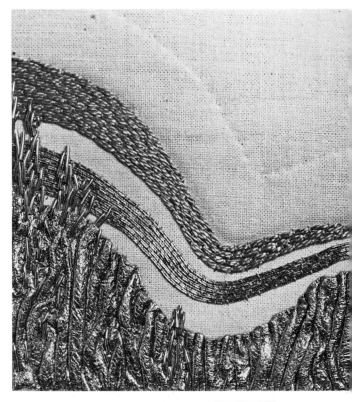

80 Very soft gloving leather which has been ruched and which is a good foil to the smooth couching and padding

81 The base of a giant pine cone which suggests rows of padded shapes attached at one edge only

82 A detail of a panel by Jan Messent showing small scraps of tweed secured with straight stitches

83 Rolled and folded paper design

RAISED EFFECTS

Texture is raised even if only slightly, and this quality can be exploited and emphasized to give depth and form. The shadows cast by the raised parts add interest and give definition to those parts. The direction from which the light will fall, and the shape of the ensuing shadows, must be taken into consideration when planning the design (figures 85 and 86).

Investigation into various ways of raising parts of the work to obtain certain results can lead to a totally three-dimensional embroidery, which has the advantage of unexpected aspects as it is viewed from different sides. When working something experimental in a raised form it is a good idea to build a mock-up of paper or card as this will solve some of the problems. The card can be scored and folded (or darted), and then it can be glued or taped to hold it in shape.

Depth can be implied, usually by the use of tone or colour, or it can be actual; there are many ways of achieving this. One of the most common, because it is so satisfactory to use giving richness and body, is quilting in its various forms. Apart from some quilting, nearly all raised effects should be worked on a backing fabric stretched on a frame to keep the raised parts from sinking back.

QUILTING

Wadded quilting (figure 87) has a layer of fabric each side of the wadding with stitching holding all three layers together. *Corded quilting* (figure 88) has a thick yarn threaded through twin lines of stitching holding the fabric and backing together. It is usually smooth, but the yarn can be pulled to leave gathers. *Stuffed quilting* (figure 89) has small raised areas with the stuffing pushed through slits cut in the backing which are then sewn up. *Shadow quilting* is produced when coloured padding shows through the top layer of fabric. This padding could be cut lengths of threads, scraps of crumpled fabric or objects.

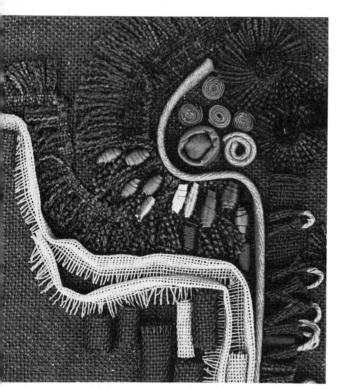

84 A fabric sampler including frayed strips, leather 'beads' and rolled fabric. The long strip of denim was glued with the edges folded into the middle, and it is stiff enough to stand on edge

85 Weathered limestone. The way the rock has been undercut in layers suggests layers of thread treatments or layers of distorted loosely woven fabric

There is no reason why two or more forms of quilting should not be used together, and any of these methods can be worked by hand or machine. Fabric can be gathered, pintucked, slit or distorted before it is quilted.

PADDING

Padding with felt or thin foam cut in increasingly smaller shapes with the largest one used on top gives a domed effect (figure 90 can be used as a basis for the design). Larger shapes need more layers of padding to give height than smaller ones, and each layer can be stuck or sewn to the backing. These padded shapes can be covered with a piece of fabric or leather cut the same shape but slightly larger; or they can be under part of a much larger piece of fabric and outlined with stitching which holds the rest of the fabric flat. Padded shapes can also be covered with threads or stitching, beads or cut purl.

Padding with string, card, corn plasters (figure 91), curtain rings, metal studs, bottle tops, packaging materials (figure 92), or anything else which raises the fabric or threads from the backing is fairly straightforward, provided it is in low relief and the fabric is not too stiff. If more height is wanted, it is better to cover a shape separately by lacing the fabric across the back of it and then by attaching it with glue or stitching. Carved polystyrene, foam or balsa wood can all be used, but it is advisable to cover them with a fabric that does not fray easily and that will mould or stretch without wrinkling. Darts, pleats and tucks can be used to make fabric fit a shape; canvas can be dampened and moulded over a shape, and then it can be left to dry. If a particular shape is too awkward to cover in one piece it can be built up in sections.

A *strip of card*, covered with fabric cut on the bias, can be sewn by one edge to a background, and it will stay upright if it is bent or curved to make shapes; this can be of varying height in one piece of work (figure 93). The roof shown in figure 94 could

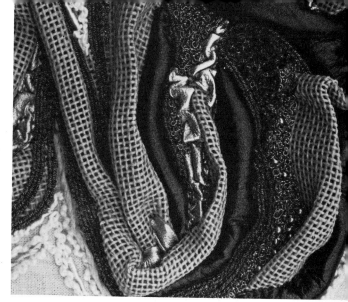

86 A fairly wide strip of canvas has been folded and sewn together before being sewn to the background. Stuffed leather strips, ruched gold kid, couching and french knots in metal thread hide the raw edges

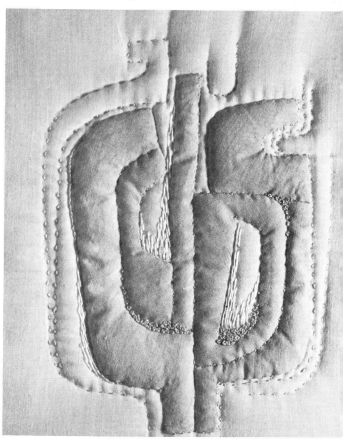

87 Wadded quilting, with appliqué to strengthen the design; the embroidery was worked through all the layers. The design is based on a flower drawing by Audrey Tucker

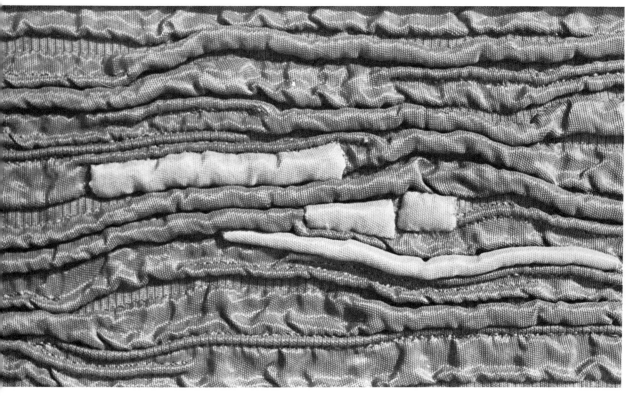

88 A form of corded quilting using rayon plissé threaded with knitting wool. The whole piece of fabric was then placed on a backing, and the fabric was distorted before it was sewn onto. This texture was suggested by a ploughed field

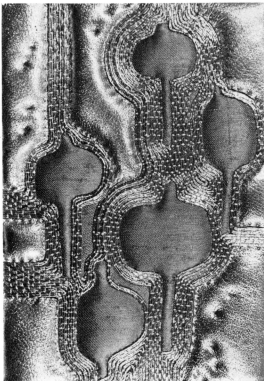

89 Stuffed quilting in a design suggested by honesty seed heads. Turquoise silk, gold kid, and couched Jap gold were used. The stuffing is animal wool which is very resilient

90 Warm wax was dropped into a tin lid half full of water, and then it was built up in layers. The wax shape was inverted, and beads and eyelets were pressed into it while still warm (Paul Harding)

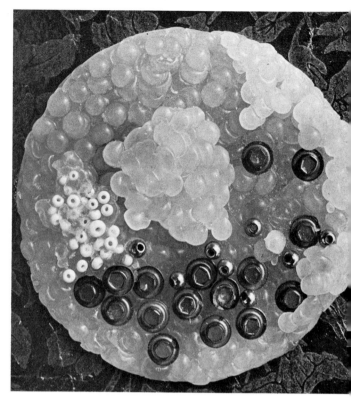

91 Sticky-backed corn plasters placed between the leather and a backing. These plasters come in a variety of shapes and sizes, and they can be cut easily

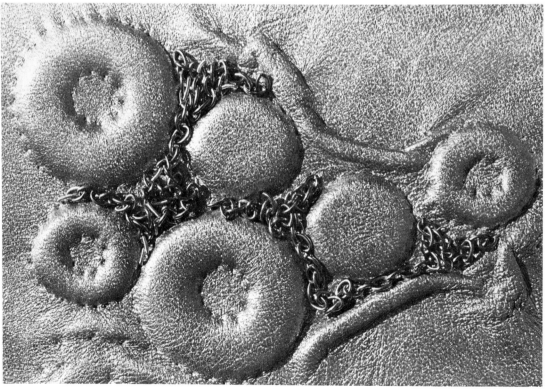

be the inspiration for this method. Fabric-covered card can also be used with the flat side facing the fabric and bent to raise the centre or one side of a shape. It should be scored first to bend in a clean line.

RAISED THREADS

Threads raised from the background cast shadows and leave space under them for other objects. Threads can be taken over beads, rings, stones, pieces of wood, cane or tubing, rolls of fabric, padded areas, buttons, string (figures 95, 96 and 97) and many other objects. Threads or stitches can be raised slightly by a padding of laid threads or a bundle of threads. An example of this is when some thick threads are couched as padding in a line, raised stem band is worked over the top of them, and then one or two rows of raised chain band are worked on top to give even more height and a change of texture.

Some stiff threads can be formed into hoops or bridges and will stay at right angles to the background. Other softer threads will collapse, but if looped in bundles and couched firmly between the loops they will give a slightly raised effect.

Stitches can be raised by working a semi-detached form of the stitch into itself rather than into the fabric and by pulling it up as it is worked. Buttonhole will do this, working the first row into a line of backstitches and succeeding rows into each other and not into the fabric even at the ends. This technique can make quite high ridges and fit any shape.

Rouleaux, wrapped threads, strips of weaving, cords, strips of fabric folded and glued to hold their shape, or stitching over lengths of string (figure 98 suggests this) or tubing can all be worked separately; then they can be attached at certain points only. Wire can be covered with threads or stitches; then it can be bent into very intricate shapes, hoops or coils and the ends poked through to the back. This sort of treatment often gives a feeling of movement as well as depth, and

these lengths can be looped, twisted or intertwined with each other.

Thread constructions can be made over moulds and then can be sewn on, leaving space under them. Sometimes the stitchery will hold the shape, but if not it could be worked over a wire frame which is left in place and which hardly shows when finished.

Very raised macramé shapes such as cylinders, worked in half-hitches, will be stiff enough to stand alone. Some threads are looped over a curtain ring, leaving one of them very much longer than the others. Half-hitches are made with each thread in turn onto the long one, working in a spiral. Extra threads can be joined on as required to vary the shape.

LAYERS

Fabric-covered card can be built up in layers as in a relief map (figure 99). The best way of doing this is to start with the smallest piece and to lace the fabric over it. It is then sewn to the next largest piece of fabric which is then laced over its card and so on.

Layers of fabric (figure 100) can be separated from each other by attaching the edges of one fabric to the back of a wooden frame and another one to the front. If the frame is thin enough more than one can be used giving many layers. If the fabric is opaque obviously holes must be cut in it to show the other layers through, but if it is transparent or loosely woven this is not necessary. With some woven materials, if some threads are withdrawn in one direction the remaining threads will fall into two layers. These layers can be treated to emphasize this, and more layers of stitching can be worked on top.

Weaving or embroidery can be worked on threads which are strung from one edge of an area to another, going in different directions, and which are worked in layers. These layers of threads can also be strung through holes bored in a wooden or metal frame. More than one of these frames can be used in a single piece of work, and they could be at different levels.

HANGING AND MOVABLE SHAPES

Loose shapes either of double fabric (which could be stuffed or stiffened) or of threads which have been wrapped or bundled can be attached at one edge only and left hanging free (figure 101).

Nets or baskets of crochet or detached buttonhole can be worked around objects like stones; then they can be attached to the background and can be left to hang. Pompoms, tassels, balls, buttonholed rings can be sewn on with the working thread, or they could slide along a rod or a cord to be moved at will.

Raised work can sometimes become too heavy and then it drags the background fabric; therefore, the lightest materials possible must be used, and a firm fabric ground must be worked on (figure 102). If the piece is to be mounted on card be sure that it is very tightly laced across the back. If it is to hang then a strong interlining will be needed to give the necessary body and to support the raised parts.

A raised effect can sometimes be carried onto the next area in a flattened version or in stitchery, which will help to integrate the two areas and to prevent the raised part from being too isolated.

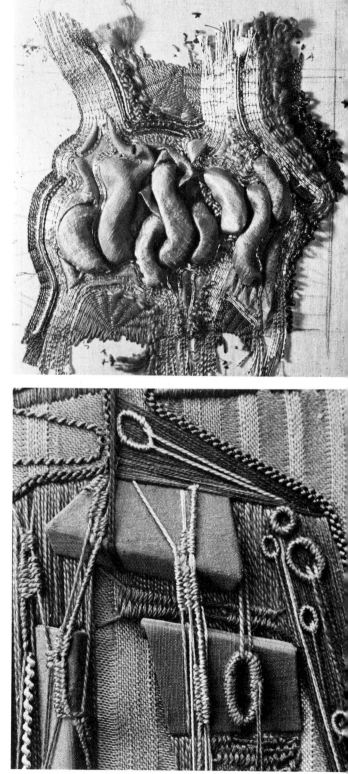

92 Polystyrene shapes, normally used as a packing material, are used here under pieces of silk cut on the cross. The surplus fabric is folded, and couching covers the raw edges. Loops were made in various threads to add texture

93 Card was scored and folded; it was covered with felt and then fabric. The raw edges are turned under, and then laced or glued

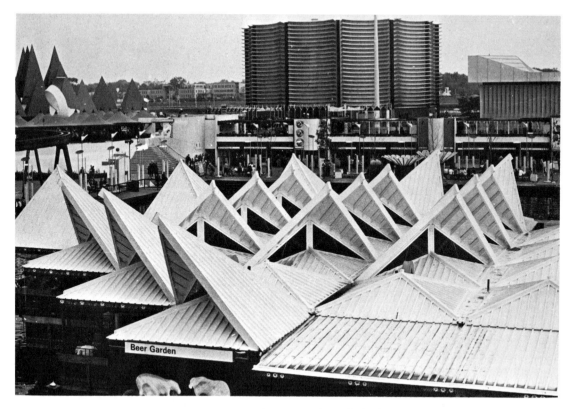

94 A roof of a building at Expo 67

95 Reflections in a river, using satin stitch over string

96 Or nue worked over felt padding. Rust and brown threads on Jap gold were used

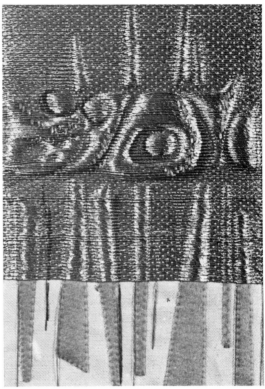

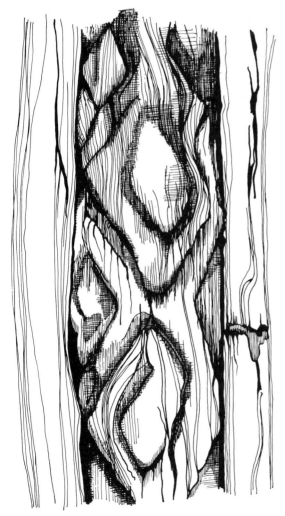

97 This drawing of a carved wooden Maori totem pole suggests threads over highly padded shapes which could be worked separately and fitted together like a jigsaw (Jan Messent)

98 A charred wooden door which suggests
raised thread constructions stiffened with glue,
or couched threads over string (Jonathan
Harding)

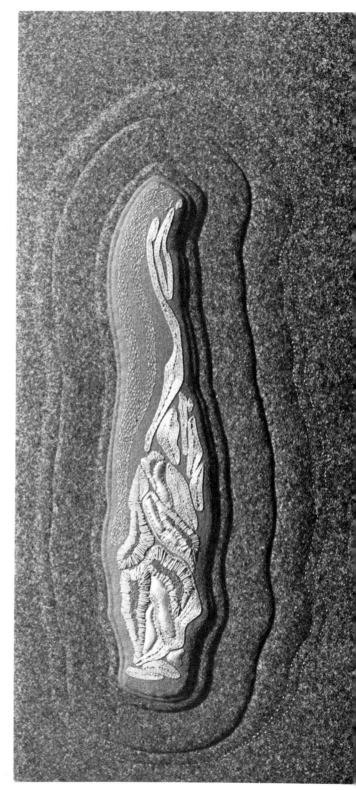

99 'Bacon' by Valerie Campbell-Harding, using
layers of fabric over card. Couched gold, cut
purl over padding, leather, and french knots
made with threads drawn from the background
fabric were also used

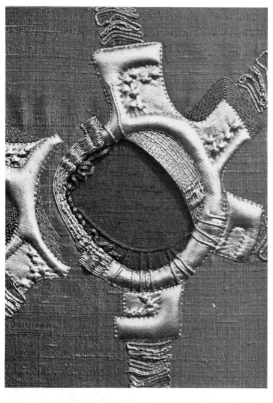

100 Part of a panel based on a broken wheel hub. Pintucks, felt and string padding, and beads placed under the leather to break the smoothness were used. The darker fabric is another layer showing through the central hole

101 *below* A petalled bathing cap. A circular shape with five petal shapes around it is cut in one flat piece. The centre circle is glued to a backing, and the petals are folded up. They are kept upright by the pressure of the shapes next to them

102 *opposite* A detail of 'Waterfall' by Jane Clarke. The leather shapes are only lightly attached, and they cast shadows. Grips of velvet are looped, and weaving is worked over the top of buttonholed ridges and other weaving

ADDING OBJECTS

Materials other than fabrics and threads can be used on an embroidery. Some objects give shine or glitter when they catch the light; some add variety in colour or texture or shape; some give depth and cast shadows. Use of non-conventional objects (figures 103, 104 and 105) is most successful when they lose their original identity and when they add to the total effect; if immediately recognizable in their own right some things look gimmicky, and probably they should not be used. There is much pleasure in searching for and finding unusual materials, but sometimes problems arise when it comes to attaching them. Necessity is often the mother of invention, and whichever method is used it should fit in with the overall scheme of the work. Very often some other technique already used in another part can be adapted to secure an object.

SOME THINGS TO USE

Beads and sequins have been in use for centuries and also bugles, pearls and jewels (figure 106). As these have holes in them there is no problem in attaching them. They need not lie flat but can be up-ended to vary the shape.

Buttons, buckles and pieces of old jewellery are easy to attach; button moulds can be used covered with either fabric or thread treatments.

Stones, crystals, pebbles, seeds and shells all pose a problem as any method of attaching them tends to distract from their beauty, and so it has to be as unobtrusive as possible. Sometimes holes can be drilled in them.

Rings and rods made of anything – metal, plastic, glass or wood – can be either left unadorned or covered with threads or stitches, or fabric (figure 107). Sometimes they can be cut and used in sections.

Metal shapes of all sorts are particularly useful (figure 108). Hooks and eyes, rings, studs, washers, chains, copper shapes for jewellery, paper clips, cogs and wheels, lids, jewellery findings and pieces of machinery can often be just what is wanted on an

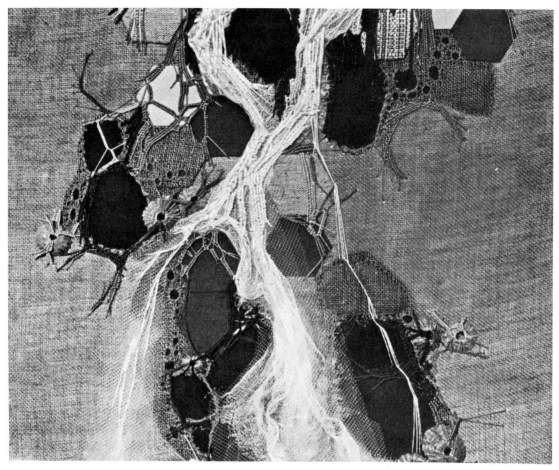

103 'My North Country II' by Jan Messent.
Gauze bandage, net, tweed, cotton and suede
were used under and on top of scrim, with
weaving, eyelets, straight stitches and shells

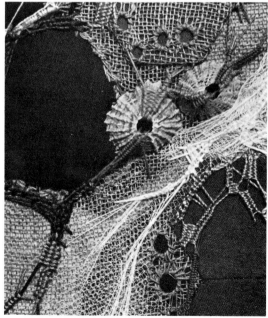

104 A detail of 'My North Country II'
showing well-scrubbed limpets with holes drilled
in them for stitching through

105 Eucalyptus bark. Pieces of this could be incorporated in an embroidery as it is soft enough to sew through

embroidery. Metal shavings, molten metal shapes and granulated zinc pieces from chemistry sets can be used in the right place.

Home-made purl, which can be larger than the ready bought gold and silver purl, is made by winding wire or thin metal, such as copper unravelled from a pot scourer, around a needle or a knitting needle.

Chunks of glass or other substances can often be the most difficult things to secure unless a hole can be drilled through them with a dentist's drill. If this is not possible a cage of threads will hold them. Sometimes a transparent nylon thread is the only one possible as sharp edges will cut other sewing threads. Strips of wood, cane, metal, leather or plastic can be held down with threads going right across them, which must be very tight otherwise the strips slip out.

Tassels, bobbles, cords or plaits can be attached by a length of thread left when making them (figure 109).

Polythene tubing is very versatile and comes in different sizes. Strips and slices can be cut from it; it can be covered with fabric, leather, or threads and stitches; coloured threads can run through it; or it can be stuffed with cut lengths of thread, pieces of fabric, small beads and so on.

SOME WAYS OF ATTACHING OBJECTS

(1) *By sewing*. Stitches can go either through holes in the object (figure 110) or right over the top of it. If the stitches are too long or if further decoration is wanted the threads can be whipped, buttonholed or woven. Overcast or buttonholed bars or stiff metal threads can make a series of hoops going over each other, under which the stone or other object can move slightly but cannot fall out. Buttonhole stitch can make small cups which will hold objects to a fabric. A row of running stitch is worked around the edge, and then rows of detached buttonhole (each one worked slightly tighter than the last) are worked into each other until it is felt that the object is secure (figure 111).

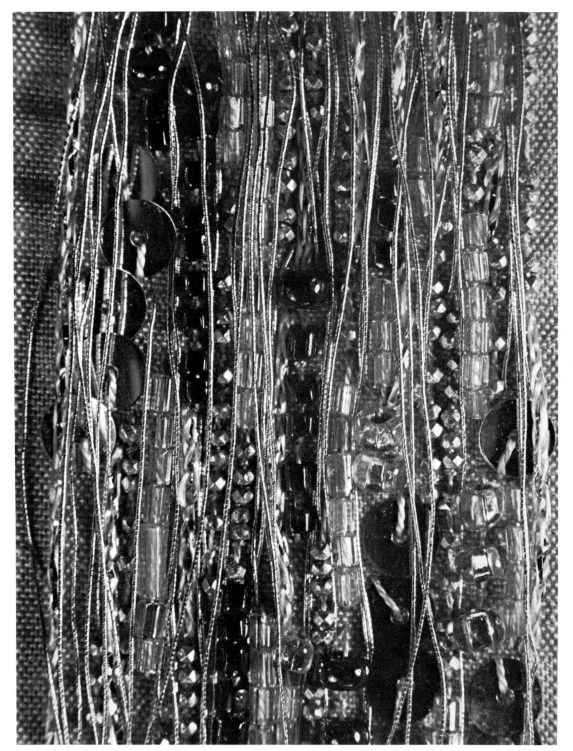

106 Long loose threads which move slightly
over beads and sequins. This was suggested by
the bark, and it could be used on dress

107 Rings, eyelets, screw collars and studs. Some of these have 'legs' which poke through to the back and which are then bent over to secure the object

108 A metal shape made by Paul Harding, who melted air gun pellets in a tin lid and then poured the liquid metal onto a stone slab. It can also be poured onto bark or other textured surfaces, and it will take an impression of them. It is held by stitching with transparent nylon thread through holes punched in the thinner spots with a large needle

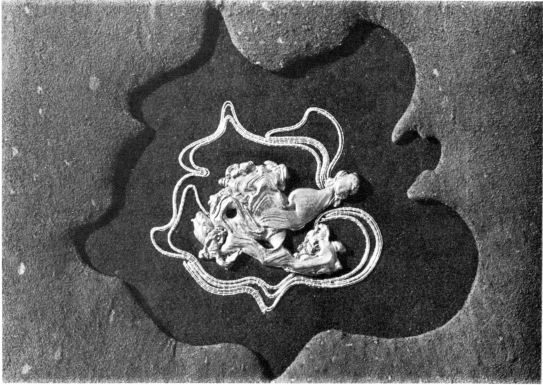

(2) *By covering* with a transparent fabric. The object can be wrapped in the fabric which is then sewn to the ground; alternatively fabric can be laid over the top and then can be stitched to the ground around the edge of the object. Use net, organdie, nylon stocking, plastic, wire mesh or anything else that allows the objects underneath to show through.

(3) *Other things can be put on top* such as a slice of tubing (figure 112) or a bead, which can be held down with threads that also anchor the object.

(4) *A cage* (figure 113) can be made over the object to be held using metal shapes; alternatively a cage or net of threads or stitches such as buttonhole or stem stitch can be worked very loosely.

Some objects look better firmly attached and immovable, and some look better when hanging or swinging. It is also possible to suspend stones or chunks of glass in a hole cut into the background. The easiest way to do this is to take threads or wire from one edge of the hole to the opposite side and back again in three or four different places. As they cross each other they can be knotted together for security on each side of the stone.

A dab of glue will often hold an unwieldy shape in place just long enough for it to be attached by some other method, but it is not strong enough to be used alone. If a piece is too unwieldy to hold with glue or a finger, a shape approximating it can be cut out of thin card and can be temporarily put in place while the foundation of a buttonhole cup (or other method) is worked; the object is then put back, and the stitching is finished.

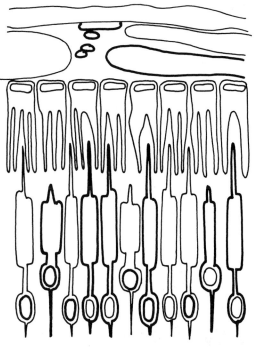

109 A drawing from a microscope slide which could be carried out using fringing, wrapped bundles of threads, tassels and hanging objects

110 A shape cut from an embossed plastic tile. It is thin enough to sew through

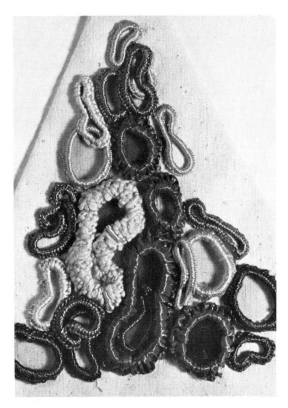

111 Buttonholed rings, worked over threads wound around the finger, can be squashed into many shapes. Here they are used to hold down pieces of coloured glass. They could be looped through each other; they could be folded over; they could have bundles of threads going through them; or they could be attached at both ends and then could be humped in the middle to hold a stone.

112 Slices of polythene tubing used to hold shi-sha. Slits were cut in the felt going outwards from the centre, and the points were raised up to leave a space for the tubing

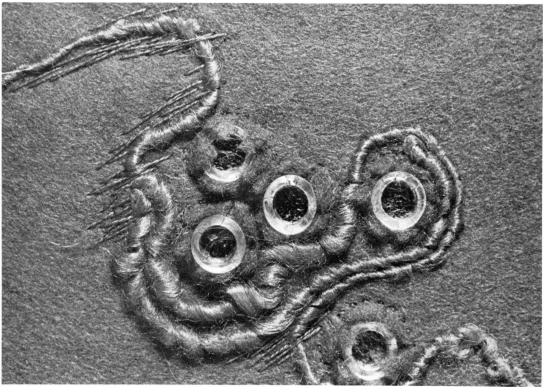

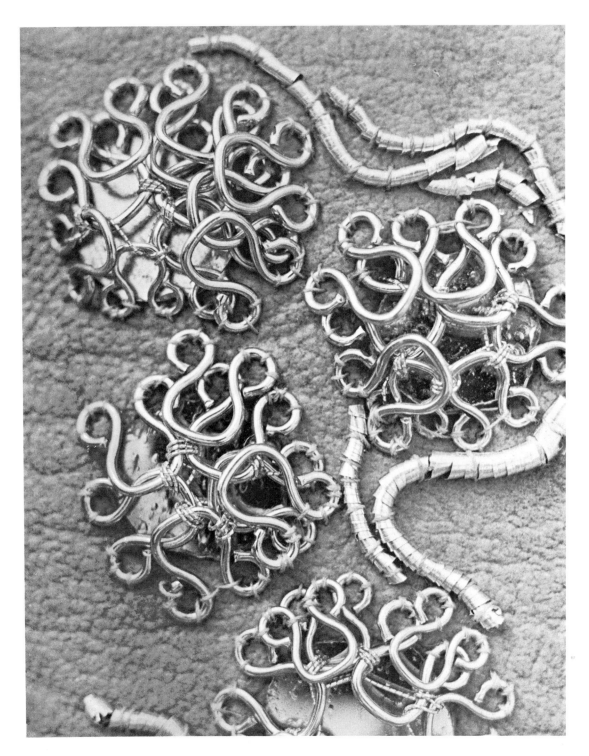

113 Cages were built up of metal eyes over
pieces of mirror, and are reflected in them.
Coiled aluminium shavings were added to
connect the shapes

CONCLUSION

Embroidery is an art form as well as a medium for decoration. It is an exciting creative activity and should be lively and original. To achieve this, constant experiment is necessary, leading to expressive interpretation. Although some of the traditional materials are not now obtainable, so much *is* available that the choice in one piece of work must be limited to avoid confusion.

Embroidery is composed of design, colour, tone and texture. All are so involved with each other that it is difficult to separate one element from the others. However, it is hoped that this book will help to encourage experimentation to achieve textures that interpret the character of the design.

UK Suppliers

The Campden Needlecraft Centre
High Street
Chipping Campden
Gloucestershire

Crown Needlework
23 High Street
Hungerford
Berkshire

de Denne Limited
159/161 Kenton Road
Kenton
Harrow
Middlesex HA3 0EU

The Handworker's Market
The Shire Hall
Holt
Norfolk NR25 6BG

Mace and Nairn
89 Crane Street
Salisbury
Wiltshire SP1 2PY

Needle and Thread
80 High Street
Horsell
Woking
Surrey

The Nimble Thimble
26 The Green
Bilton
Rugby CV22 7LY

Christine Riley
53 Barclay Street
Stonehaven
Kincardineshire AB3 2AR

The Royal School of Needlework
25 Princes Gate
London SW7 1QE

Silken Strands
33 Linksway
Gatley
Cheadle
Cheshire

The Silver Thimble
33 Gay Street
Bath
Avon BA1 2NT

Yarncraft
112A Westbourne Grove
London W2 5RU

USA Suppliers

Appleton Brothers of London
West Main Road
Little Compton
Rhode Island 02837

American Crewel Studio
Box 298
Boonton
New Jersey 07005

American Thread Corporation
90 Park Avenue
New York

Bucky King Embroideries
Box 371
King Bros
3 Ranch Buffalo Star Rte
Sheriden
Wyoming 82801

The Thread Shed
307 Freeport Road
Pittsburgh
Pennsylvania 15215

INDEX